Original title:
What's Life Without a Little Humor?

Copyright © 2025 Creative Arts Management OÜ
All rights reserved.

Author: Evelyn Hartman
ISBN HARDBACK: 978-1-80566-004-0
ISBN PAPERBACK: 978-1-80566-299-0

The Tickle of Tomorrow

In the morning, I tripped on my shoe,
Laughed so hard, I forgot what to do.
Chasing my coffee, it danced on the floor,
Guess that's what mornings are truly for!

The cat wore a hat, looked quite absurd,
Chirping like birds, it was simply unheard.
A squirrel by the window, a pop quiz for me,
Who knew they could mimic and act like a spree?

The sun peeked in, with a wink and a grin,
Telling me, "Hey, let the giggles begin!"
So I wobbled outside with a fumble and cheer,
Life's too short not to laugh, that's quite clear!

In the evening, I danced with the moon,
Spinning and twirling, a comical tune.
So here's to the moments that shine bright with glee,
For joy is the spark that sets laughter free!

Sassy Smirks and Snorts

In a world where silliness reigns,
The cat plays chess, ignoring the pains.
With giggles that tickle the air,
We dance like no one would dare.

Oh, a pratfall here, a wink over there,
Life's slapstick moments light as a flare.
Banter that bounces, laughter that flies,
We jest with our hearts, humor our prize.

Try not to chuckle, I dare you to pause,
As grandmas tell jokes with applause.
A wink and a nudge, the world spins in glee,
Smirks and snorts, oh, how sweetly they be!

So gather your friends for a throw of confetti,
In the realm of jest, we remain all setty.
With every giggle, there's wisdom we earn,
For joy is the fire, and laughter, the burn.

Mirthful Echoes

Echoes of laughter bounce off the walls,
As we chase after joy wherever it calls.
With jests like confetti that float in the breeze,
Every silly moment does just as it please.

A pratfall in motion, we double in glee,
As puppies in hats play at tea with a bee.
The howls of the crowd, with laughter so loud,
Unraveling giggles, we feel so proud.

With pranks piled high, oh, what fun it brings,
As clowns rob the seriousness of their wings.
We dance on the edge of the absurd and bright,
In this circus of joy, all hearts take flight.

So, raise up your voice, let the echoes resound,
In a world of silliness, laughter is found.
With every good jest, we grant ourselves cheer,
Life's fun little secrets make everything clear.

The Glee of the Unforeseen

Surprises await just around the next bend,
A banana peel lurking, ready to send.
With belly laughs bubbling, we tumble with grace,
Finding joy in the moments we sometimes misplace.

The unexpected giggles from a wandering breeze,
Make mischief and mayhem feel like sweet teasing.
With oops and oh no, we relish the ride,
In this playful dance, we take humor in stride.

Let's toast to the folly, the quirks that we share,
With wisecracks and punchlines that fill up the air.
For every mishap that leads us to grin,
Is a lesson in laughter, a chance to begin.

So wander with joy into chaos and fun,
Embrace every twist, for it's never quite done.
In the glee of the unforeseen, laughter ignites,
A symphony of chuckles, our hearts take flight.

Capturing the Comical

With a camera in hand, let's capture the jest,
Moments of humor, we treasure the best.
Faces that crinkle, with laughter so bright,
The essence of joy, in candid delight.

The dad joke's embrace, a tickle to the ears,
A pie to the face, oh, our laughter appears.
We freeze every giggle, encase every smile,
To relive the joy, let's stay for a while.

Amidst all the nonsense, we collect every tale,
Crafting a tapestry where silliness prevails.
From hiccups to snorts in the fabric of day,
We find humor's magic in playful display.

So let's weave our stories where laughter can thread,
In the quilt of our lives, let humor be spread.
For humor's a treasure, a gift to impart,
Capturing the comical, the joy of the heart.

Chortles in the Moonlight

Beneath the glow of silver beams,
Laughter dances in our dreams.
Stars tickle truth with cheeky glee,
Joyful whispers swirl for free.

A cat in boots does pirouettes,
While silly ponds host fishy pets.
The night is bright with jolly jest,
A playful heart is truly blessed.

Spirited Silliness

A marching band of bees in hats,
Play hopscotch with the neighborhood cats.
Rainbows wear mismatched socks,
Giggles bloom like polka-dots.

In a world where bananas skate,
And silly ducks debate their fate.
The coffee's brewed with a wink and sigh,
Who needs a reason? Just let it fly!

The Comedy of Life's Curves

Life's a ride on a rollercoaster,
With every dip, we laugh and foster.
A pie in the face, what a sweet surprise,
We learn to smile through messy cries.

The bubbles burst but joy remains,
Like dancing raindrops on windowpanes.
Witty jabs and playful rhymes,
Life's a stand-up show, with perfect times.

Frivolities and Fables

Once a fish told tales so grand,
Of treasure hunts on a sandy land.
With seaweed wigs and shells for crowns,
Their joy could flip the fiercest frowns.

A dog recites the news of squirrels,
While the wind plays tricks with laughing curls.
In this quirky tale of whimsy bright,
We find our hearts in pure delight.

Cheeky Cheeriness

A grin that stretches wide and bright,
Giggles dance on wings of light.
When troubles knock, a joke takes flight,
Laughter's spark ignites the night.

In kitchen chaos, laughter spills,
A cat in mittens makes the thrills.
Whiskers twitch as humor fills,
Life's a jest, it surely drills.

Sunny skits of every day,
In awkward moments, we can play.
A clownish slip or silly sway,
In joyful hearts, we find our way.

So wear a smile, it suits you best,
In cheeky cheer, we'll jest and jest.
With every chuckle, we invest,
A life well-lived is truly blessed.

Puns in the Petals

In gardens where the daisies joke,
A pun blooms bright with every poke.
Roses whisper, 'We're thorny folk!'
While violets smile, never broke.

The sunflowers bask in golden cheer,
'You're looking tall,' they slyly leer.
A merry breeze, a friend so near,
Their laughter floats, it's crystal clear.

Lilies laugh, their petals sway,
'We've got blooms to brighten your day!'
With every giggle, woes decay,
Nature's humor leads the way.

So next time that your heart feels flat,
Remember, life's a little chat.
With puns and petals, fancy that,
A joyful dance with nature's brat.

Jestful Journeys

On winding roads, the laughter flows,
With silly hats and comical clothes.
Adventures start where humor glows,
In every heart, a chuckle grows.

We trip on toes and land in mud,
Spilling snacks, oh what a flood!
With every blunder, joy will thud,
In jestful travels, life's not a dud.

Maps of laughter lead us far,
To funny towns, where gags are star.
With wacky signs and a quirky car,
Our happy hearts, no need to spar.

So pack a grin, we're on our way,
The road is bright, come join the play.
With jestful journeys, come what may,
Laughter guides us, come seize the day!

The Cracks that Create

In every crack, a joke may hide,
A wobbly chair can't run and bide.
With every stumble, smile with pride,
For humor blooms where quirks reside.

A shattered pot may still hold dreams,
In broken places, joy redeems.
In every mishap, laughter beams,
Life's comic play, or so it seems.

We trip and fall, but here's the plan,
Each fall reveals a funny span.
From silly slips, we'll dance and span,
In every moment, laughter can.

So cherish cracks that bring delight,
In flaws and foibles, humor's light.
With every giggle, our spirits height,
Makes life a canvas, bold and bright.

Silliness as a Survival Tool

In wobbly shoes, we dance through the day,
With jellybeans bouncing, we laugh all the way.
A penguin in pajamas, a cat in a hat,
Life's lighthearted moments, just think of that.

With every odd giggle, we wiggle and twirl,
Juggling our worries, giving life a whirl.
Tickle the fancies, let silliness reign,
For laughter's the treasure we find in the rain.

Whimsy at Dawn

Morning breaks softly with giggles and glee,
Sunshine tickles the flowers, joyful and free.
A squirrel wearing glasses sips tea by the tree,
Whimsy awakens, as bright as can be.

The toast starts to dance, the eggs sing a song,
In a world full of laughter, where all things belong.
Every moment a chuckle, a smile just erupts,
As the day opens wide with silliness pumped.

Laughter Like Morning Coffee

Rich aroma of humor fills the air each day,
Like coffee in the morning, it keeps gloom at bay.
A spoonful of grin mixed with giggles so bright,
Sippin' laughter for breakfast, sets everything right.

In the grind of the day, just brew up some fun,
Watch worries dissolve as the humor's begun.
Mugs raised to the sky, let the joy overflow,
Life's brew, steeped in laughter, just watch it glow.

Finding Rainbows in the Routine

From chores to the dishes, we stir up some cheer,
A broomstick can dance, if you let it steer.
Dancing through laundry, we kick up our heels,
Finding bright colors in mundane meals.

A simple old schedule is now filled with fun,
Spinning our days like a game to be won.
With each little chuckle, the routine shifts hue,
Painting our lives in shades of laughter anew.

The Art of Joyful Nonsense

In a world of quirks and giggles,
We dance like ducks on wiggly wiggles.
A cat that sings, a fish that prances,
Life's too short, let's take our chances.

Socks that don't match, a hat askew,
Giggling at jokes that are silly, it's true.
Why not jest, and play the fool,
For laughter's the best, the golden rule.

With joy on our lips and sparkles in eyes,
We twirl in the rain beneath gray skies.
An umbrella turns into a flying kite,
Oh, the wonders of a pure delight!

So when the day feels heavy and long,
Remember the power of a silly song.
A tickle, a chuckle, let worries cease,
In nonsense we find a joyful peace.

Laughter in the Shadows

Whispers of chuckles hide in the night,
Where shadows dance in the soft moonlight.
An old shoe laughs as it trips on a stone,
The world is a stage where whimsy is grown.

In corners, the echoes of giggles arise,
As dreams take flight and paint the skies.
A puppy's leap or a clumsy fall,
Every little fumble is a funny call.

When troubles come knocking, take out your jokes,
The best kind of banter is what laughter invokes.
With friends by your side and a grin on your face,
Even the dullest moments can find their grace.

For jesters of joy carry light in their hearts,
With every pun, the darkness departs.
So conjure a smile, let the shadows disperse,
Laughter is magic, it's the universe's curse!

Jests of the Everyday

A spoon that sings, a fork that prances,
Every meal's a chance for funny chances.
When life gives you lemons, dance in the rain,
Pour sugar and laughter to soften the pain.

Waking up late with mismatched shoes,
The cat in the mirror has the best views.
Coffee spills over, a dance on the floor,
In all of this chaos, let's aim for more.

Silly hats worn to brighten the day,
Turn mundane moments into a ballet.
A slip on a banana, a pie to the face,
In every mishap, we find our place.

So grab a good joke, pull up a chair,
Let's laugh in the breeze, float light as air.
For life is a jest, a glorious spree,
With every good laugh, we set our hearts free.

The Wit We Wear

Wit is our armor, laughter our shield,
In the battle of life, joy is revealed.
A smile is fierce, a bright shining star,
With humor, our burdens feel lighter by far.

From whiskers on puppies to gaffes in the mall,
Life's very essence is a good-natured brawl.
With playful jibes and a wink of the eye,
We conquer our worries as we pass them by.

Chasing a toddler who's running amok,
Stepping on Legos, oh, what bad luck!
But every small blunder, a tale we will tell,
With laughter as music, our hearts ring a bell.

So let's wear our wit like a colorful dress,
Adorned with the joys and the silly excess.
In the theater of life, play the lead role,
For laughter's the heartbeat that nourishes the soul.

Silly Serenades

In the morning, a toast to the bread,
With jelly that dances, it's never quite spread.
A cat in a hat, oh what a delight,
Chasing its tail till it takes flight.

Beneath the bright sun, the dog plays fetch,
With socks from the dryer, a curious sketch.
Laughs echo louder, the birds sing along,
It's a world of giggles, where everyone belongs.

Banter Beneath the Surface

In the pool, a frog does a splashy dive,
Wearing tiny goggles, it feels so alive.
With each little croak, it cracks up the crowd,
Even the goldfish giggles out loud.

A snail in a race, now that's quite absurd,
Zooming past turtles—oh, haven't you heard?
With a wink and a grin, they finish the game,
In this world of silliness, nothing's the same.

Jokes that Jump

A horse walks into a bar, gets a drink,
The bartender chuckles, can you even think?
When asked why he's here, with a smirk so sly,
He says, 'For the hay, and to see the sky.'

A chicken on roller skates flaps with a cheer,
Who knew it could skate? Let's give it a year.
With laughter so bright, they twirl through the day,
In this circus of life, come join the ballet.

Quips from a Quiet Corner

In a quiet little nook, a mouse tells a joke,
While nibbling on cheese, it starts to provoke.
A shadow of laughter creeps under the door,
Even the cat chuckles, can't ignore.

An old teddy bear sits with his wise little grin,
Says, 'Life's a plush ride, don't forget to spin.'
Each wrinkle tells stories of laughter and glee,
In this haven of quirks, we're all meant to be.

Eccentricities of Existence

In a world full of quirks and cheer,
Laughter bubbles, bright and clear.
Cats in hats and shoes on dogs,
Dance through life like playful frogs.

Shadows stretch but don't you frown,
Slips and tumbles turn you 'round.
With each slip, a laugh will fly,
Finding joy in the awkward try.

The Jest-ful Spirit

Tickling ribs with jest and glee,
A playful wink, a silly spree.
Grumpy gnomes and wisecrack birds,
Life's a canvas, use the words.

Giggles sprout like flowers wild,
Every grown-up, still a child.
In every laugh, a spark ignites,
Turning troubles into delights.

Sly Smiles in the Storm

Raindrops dance, but worry not,
A puddle's splash will hit the spot.
Umbrellas flipped, a scene of fun,
With every slip, a new day's done.

Winds may gust and tempests roar,
Yet in the chaos, we laugh more.
Sly smiles hide, but never fade,
For mirth is where true hearts are laid.

Nuances of Nonsense

Fluffy clouds in a bright pink sky,
Why not question, and wonder why?
Dancing spoons and chatting chairs,
Life's most fun in curious stares.

Juggling pies with silly ease,
Puns and giggles, just to tease.
In every oddball twist and turn,
Laughter's glow is what we yearn.

Grins in Gray Moments

When clouds roll in and skies turn dark,
A little joke can leave a mark.
A slip on ice, a sudden trip,
Laughter's the vessel; joy's the ship.

Embrace the blunders, they make us whole,
A clumsy dance can soothe the soul.
With every mishap, we share a grin,
Happiness found in the chaos within.

Lemons can be sweet when served with zest,
Finding joy in mess is always best.
In a world where frowns seem to parade,
A giggle's the light that won't ever fade.

So when life's a jest, take the punchline,
A giggle, a snort, let the chuckles intertwine.
For in the gray, we find our spark,
Humor's the glow that ignites the dark.

Whimsical Whispers

Whispers of joy dance in the air,
Tickling your thoughts, letting you dare.
A cat in a hat, a frog with a tune,
Life's richer with laughter; that's the boon.

Stumbles and tumbles, oh what a sight,
When we trip and fall, it feels just right.
Jokes on the lips and smiles on our face,
Turn every moment into a race.

The silliest stories make hearts collide,
A dash of whimsy, let's all take a ride.
For in every giggle, a tale will restart,
A treasure of joy in this wild work of art.

So gather the laughter, let spirits soar,
In a world of whimsy, there's always more.
With every chuckle, we paint the scene,
Life's best moments, always between.

Merriment in Mayhem

Mayhem surrounds, yet laughter breaks free,
With every misstep, our spirits agree.
A juggling act gone wrong, what a show,
In chaos, we find a joyful flow.

Trips down the stairs can make us roar,
A twist of fate, who could ask for more?
Life's little blunders bring us together,
In the storm of laughter, we laugh forever.

When the world feels heavy and full of dread,
Just recall the moments when silliness led.
A dance-off in the kitchen, what a scene,
Flour on the floor, and we're all on a team.

So embrace the madness, let spirits lift,
For merriment's magic is the greatest gift.
In the midst of mayhem, find your cheer,
Laugh through the chaos, hold your loved ones near.

Follies of the Heart

Oh, the follies of love, a comic play,
Where hearts do stumble, but laughter will stay.
A wink gone awry, a misplaced kiss,
In the theater of love, there's always bliss.

With each love letter, some ink may smear,
Yet the words of affection bring the heart near.
A bouquet of bloopers, a sweet serenade,
In the blush of romance, joy's not delayed.

When passion ignites, and the sparks fly high,
Foolish escapades make us laugh and sigh.
In the dance of affection, with twirls and spins,
The follies we share are where true love begins.

So cherish the moments of laughter and cheer,
In this whimsical journey, hold loved ones near.
For the heart finds comedy in every refrain,
In the follies of love, joy shall remain.

Frivolous Fancies

A cat in a hat with a laugh, oh so spry,
Dances with shadows as they flutter by.
Jelly beans jumping and beans that sing,
Life's just a circus when you let joy swing.

Socks mismatched on a sunny day,
Chasing the clouds that wish to play.
Umbrellas twirl in the afternoon breeze,
Laughter erupts, oh, with such ease!

Pies in the sky and dreams on the ground,
Mirth wraps around all that can be found.
With giggles that sparkle like stars in the night,
A world full of whimsy, oh what a sight!

Fun like a bubble that floats on a whim,
Tickling toes in the water so dim.
Life's little fancies, they come and they go,
Yet chase every chuckle, let happiness flow.

The Heart's Laughter

When life serves a lemon and you make it a pie,
With cream on your nose, oh, my, how you fly!
Dancing through puddles with splashes of cheer,
Whistling a tune that draws friends near.

A frog in a suit gives a wink and a ribbit,
While squirrels in bowties hold a grand visit.
Through tickles and giggles, the joy multiplies,
Even grumpy old toads can't help but guise.

Jokes in a jar waiting to burst,
Each chuckle a drop, oh, we thirst!
As laughter ripples like waves on the sea,
Embrace every chuckle, so wild and so free.

In the garden of folly, we cultivate glee,
With sunflowers swaying in perfect decree.
Gather 'round, friends, hear the heart's merry tune,
For joy is the language of sun and of moon.

Grins and Giggles

A snail wearing glasses has sights set for fun,
While ants throw a party under the sun.
The world spins around with a wobbly grin,
It's easy to dance when life lets you spin.

Balloons float by with mischief to share,
Juggling their echoes in the warm summer air.
A dog in a tutu takes center stage,
With laughter bursting forth, whatever the age.

Silly hats bouncing on heads oh so bright,
Chasing down fireflies that flicker at night.
With every good jest that adorns our stay,
Life's a parade when you laugh on the way.

From tickles of children to cheer from the wise,
We find all our joy in the simplest ties.
So grab hold of laughter, let it unite,
For smiles and giggles make everything bright.

The Jovial Journey

Off on a quest with a map made of dreams,
Finding lost treasures in laughter's sweet streams.
Ticklish adventures with friends by your side,
Swinging on moonbeams, oh how we glide!

Each corner we turn, there's a joke waiting there,
With whoopee cushions and mischievous flair.
Through valleys of chuckles and mountains of glee,
We wander together, oh what company!

The clouds have popcorn, the sun wears a grin,
With every new story, our joy just begins.
A carnival ride on the breeze of delight,
We savor each moment, each giggle ignites.

So pack up your laughter, let the fun unfold,
In the pages of life, let the stories be told.
For every adventure is brighter with cheer,
Join in the journey, where humor draws near.

A Splash of Sarcasm

Why did the chicken cross the road?
To avoid my terrible joke.
I asked the snail for a ride,
He laughed and said, 'No way, bloke!'

Every pun is a puzzle,
With laughter as the key.
When jokes are like bubble gum,
You chew, then spit with glee.

Life's a circus and so grand,
With clowns that trip and fall.
We juggle our best blunders,
As laughter echoes through the hall.

So raise a glass of snark,
To the folly we embrace.
In the comedy of mishaps,
We'll always find our place.

Wit and Wonder

A frog in a tuxedo,
What a curious sight!
He waltzed across my garden,
Under the moonlight.

With a grin that stretched real wide,
He croaked a cheerful tune.
Even stars laughed along,
As they danced with the moon.

Don't take life too serious,
With all its silly strife.
A wink and a quick quip,
Can make a better life.

So sprinkle joy like confetti,
And wear your quirkiest grin.
For the world is a playground,
And laughter's where we win.

The Silver Lining of Snickers

There once was a cat with a hat,
Who fancied himself quite smart.
He'd outwit the mouse in a duel,
But forgot where he'd parked his heart.

A cow jumped over the moon,
But fell into a pie.
She chuckled, 'What a fine meal!
I didn't mean to fly.'

With each stumble or trip,
Life's a delightful spree.
If you slip on a banana peel,
Stop to giggle with glee.

So here's to silly moments,
To snickers low and loud.
In the comedy of life,
Let's laugh to make us proud.

Laughter, the Best Medicine

A bee wore suspenders with style,
Buzzing around with delight.
He told me, 'I'm here for the honey,
Not to start a buzz fight!'

With each joke that we share,
Our worries start to fade.
A tickle, a pun, a quip,
In laughter, fears are slayed.

So here's to the clowns and the fun,
To the quirks we can't outgrow.
Let's embrace the giggles,
And dance like no one knows.

In the grand scheme of this play,
Punchlines are our fallbacks.
In the lightness of humor,
We'll dance through life's cul-de-sacs.

Humor's Harmony

Laughter bubbles like a stream,
Tickles and giggles, a joyful theme.
Every mishap, a chance to cheer,
A wink and a grin, bringing good near.

Bananas slipping in a grocery race,
Falling down with a comical grace.
Life's little quirks, a dance we share,
Finding the fun in moments rare.

Splashed by puddles on rainy days,
Witty banter in countless ways.
Jokes and jests paint smiles bright,
Turning the mundane into pure delight.

So here's to chuckles, both loud and small,
In every stumble, let laughter call.
For in each moment, sweet and absurd,
The joy of humor is always heard.

Playful Perspectives

A cat in a hat, oh what a sight,
Using the floor as a launchpad for flight.
With silly antics, they steal the show,
Making us laugh, letting joy grow.

A child's wide eyes, full of surprise,
As silly faces make the world wise.
Tickling toes with every tale,
In this joyful game, we shall not fail.

Banter with friends over silly jokes,
Unexpected laughs from outrageous folks.
Each quip and pun helps us unwind,
In playful perspectives, happiness finds.

So let's embrace this silly dance,
Finding the humor in fate's strange chance.
For laughter's the glue that binds us tight,
In every moment, it ignites the light.

Comedy in the Commonplace

From spilled coffee to socks astray,
Life's little goofs make our day.
A mismatched pair and a fleeting glance,
Turns the ordinary into a dance.

The neighbor's dog with a flair for the stage,
Chasing its tail like a comical page.
In everyday scenes, we find the fun,
A laugh shared is brighter than the sun.

Mistaken texts, a voice turned around,
In these moments, true humor is found.
Life's little blunders, a playful tease,
Bringing us joy and warm, hearty ease.

So here's to the mischief that brightens the hours,
Lifting our spirits like blossoming flowers.
In this comedy, strange and divine,
We find the laughter that's truly mine.

Delightful Drolleries

In mismatched shoes that tell a tale,
Of droll adventures where dreams set sail.
Wobbly bikes on the street we roam,
Finding the fun wherever we comb.

A joke on the lips just waiting to pop,
The giggles contagious, they never stop.
Silly hats worn to a formal bash,
Turning the serious into a splash.

With quirks and laughter, we twirl and spin,
Under the glow of life's crazy din.
In delightful drolleries, we find our cheer,
Gathering smiles that draw us near.

So raise a glass to the silly and fun,
For in the laughter, we've all just won.
Life's a joke that's best when shared,
In drolleries sweet, happiness is aired.

Bright Blooms of Banter

In a garden where laughter grows,
Petals of giggles bloom and glow.
Bees buzzing with playful cheer,
Making each moment sweet and clear.

Clouds pass with a silly face,
Sunbeams dance in a merry race.
Nature's winks, a joyful tease,
Life's a jest, so take your ease.

The trees exchange whispers of fun,
A squirrel's dance on the run.
Every branch sways with a grin,
Inviting all to join in the spin.

So let's paint the world with delight,
Chasing shadows with bursts of light.
For in this realm of jesting blooms,
Laughter's perfume forever looms.

Tickle Your Senses

A tickle here, a sprinkle there,
Life's a game we love to share.
With every joke, a spark ignites,
Turning the mundane into delights.

Giggling gnomes on garden posts,
They cheer and jest, they laugh the most.
With every pun, a chuckle flies,
Creating joy beneath the skies.

Bubbles of laughter burst and sway,
Frolicking thoughts at play all day.
When troubles knock, we counteract,
With humor's charm, we'll never lack.

So take a leap, join the spree,
Let silly moments set you free.
In every tickle, in every jest,
Life's a party, so feel your best!

Laugh Lines of Love

With every wrinkle our smiles create,
Love's laughter ages, but never abates.
In shared glances, humor flows,
Binding our hearts in joyous prose.

Silly squabbles over the remote,
Tickling each other, we happily gloat.
In warmth and jest, with playful sighs,
We paint our lives with sweet surprise.

Over dinner, a quirky fight,
Who's the best chef? It's pure delight!
The taste of laughter, spice of the day,
Seasoned with love, come what may.

Through ups and downs, we find our way,
Our laughter's language lets us play.
For in this realm where humor thrives,
We weave a tale that forever jives.

Jests and Joys

In a world filled with playful pranks,
We dance on air, as humor thanks.
With every chuckle, stress takes flight,
Jests awaken our hearts to light.

A cat in a hat, prancing around,
Brings giggles and gasps, such joy is found.
With a wink and a nudge, we share the cheer,
Unraveling laughter, bringing us near.

Silly songs spill from the skies,
Tickling ears with sweet surprise.
In every jest, a moment bright,
Guiding us through the endless night.

So gather round and let joy flow,
In laughter's circle, love will grow.
For in our hearts, the truth we know,
Jests and joys will always glow.

A Chuckle in the Breeze

A cat in a hat, oh what a sight,
Strutting down the street, feeling just right.
With every soft step, he twirls and spins,
Drawing smiles from faces, where laughter begins.

A squirrel steals snacks, wearing a frown,
Dodging the dog as he runs through the town.
Chasing his tail, oh what a grand race,
While giggles erupt from the wide-eyed place.

A bird on a wire, sings off-key tunes,
Dancing on breezes beneath lazy moons.
Each chirp and each flap, a joke from the sky,
Lifting our spirits and making us sigh.

So let's share a laugh, with old and with new,
For joy's in the cracks where the sunshine slips through.
With chuckles and grins, life's brighter, you see,
A merry reminder of whimsy and glee.

The Lighthearted Spectrum

Colors of laughter paint skies so bright,
Yellow sunbeams tickle with light.
Blue waves of giggles roll onto the shore,
Every splash becomes fun we adore.

In the green of the grass, a hopscotch parade,
Jumping and skipping, oh the laughs we've made.
With each joyful leap, our worries take flight,
The paintbrush of humor makes everything right.

Orange sunsets wrap us in warmth,
While pink clouds giggle as they gently swarm.
Twirling like ribbons, our spirits ascend,
In this carnival of joy, there's no end.

So grab your best colors, let laughter unfold,
In every sweet moment, new stories are told.
With cheers that resound, let's dance in delight,
Together we'll shine, through day and through night.

Whimsical Whispers of Joy

A planning raccoon with his trusty map,
Looks for adventure, in a little mishap.
With breadcrumbs as treasure, he sets off to seek,
A party of friends, oh how they'll squeak!

An ant in a suit, with a briefcase galore,
Marches to meetings, Knocks on the door.
With tiny ambitions, he proudly declares,
'Let's build tiny towers, if anyone dares!'

The moon wears pajamas, tucked in so tight,
Winking at stars, it chuckles goodnight.
As dreams bounce around like balloons in the air,
Every giggle and sigh dances with care.

So gather your giggles, your chuckles, your cheer,
Let's savor the laughter that brings us near.
In whispers of joy, let the magic ensue,
For life is much richer when we're silly and true.

Laughter's Serenade

In the garden of jest, a bouquet of glee,
Flowers that giggle, soft as can be.
With petals of puns, they sway in the breeze,
Tickling our senses, aiming to please.

A turtle in shades, slow but so wise,
Chasing a rabbit who's just full of lies.
With a hop and a skip, they dance in delight,
Turning ordinary days into pure starlight.

The fish in the pond, they bubble with cheer,
Telling tales of the worms that they fear.
As ripples of laughter break onto the shore,
Each splash is a story that beckons for more.

So gather around, let's sing this sweet song,
In laughter's embrace, where we all belong.
With rhythms of joy, let our spirits all sway,
For humor's a treasure, in every ballet.

Radiance in Ridicule

In a world where blunders bloom,
Clumsy dances fill the room.
Laughter echoes loud and clear,
A joyful heart brings warmth and cheer.

Chasing dreams on wobbly feet,
Jokes and giggles can't be beat.
Every stumble's just a show,
As silly tales begin to flow.

A dog in socks, what a sight!
Bellyaches from laughing all night.
With every slip, a chance to grin,
Who knew mischief could be this win?

In laughter's glow, we find our light,
Wit and whimsy, pure delight.
Embrace the quirks, let worries flee,
Radiance shines in absurdity.

Crazy Capers

Juggling lemons on a whim,
Clowns in a race, life on a brim.
Slips on banana peels galore,
Every laugh opens a door.

A cat in shades sips iced tea,
A silly sight, oh can't you see?
With kooky hats and goofy hands,
We spread our joy across the lands.

A squirrel steals lunch with great finesse,
Each day unfolds a new jest.
From pratfalls to quirky plots,
Life's a stage, but bring your thoughts!

Through crazy capers we discover,
That overthinking leads to cover.
Let's dance through life with playful hearts,
For every laugh is where fun starts.

Unscripted Chuckles

In a world of scripted scenes,
Let joy run wild in silly dreams.
Unexpected gigs and guffaws,
Life's vibrant show without a pause.

A mishap here, a slip with flair,
Unplanned laughter fills the air.
Bloopers of life, come take a seat,
Every moment, a ticklish treat.

Impromptu dances on city streets,
Joyous faces and happy beats.
Tiny mishaps and grand designs,
Life's best moments without confines.

With every chuckle, we ignite,
The spark of joy, a pure delight.
So here's to moments unrefined,
Where laughter dances, intertwined.

Humor Under the Stars

Under the blanket of twinkling light,
Tales of laughter take their flight.
Whimsical jokes and funny fables,
Stars twinkle bright on our tiny tables.

A giggle shared beneath the moon,
In the night, we find our tune.
Dancing shadows, stories spun,
Find the joy; we've all won.

Falling off chairs in a fit of glee,
As laughter flows, we feel so free.
With every joke, the night grows warm,
Together in humor, together we swarm.

So let's raise a glass under the sky,
Cheers to laughter, oh my oh my!
With hope and giggles in every heart,
Life's a stage, let the fun start.

Whimsy on a Wednesday

A cat in a hat, oh what a sight,
Chasing after shadows in the soft moonlight.
With socks on his paws, he struts with flair,
Wobbling and bobbling, do we even care?

A pancake flips high, lands right on the floor,
The dog looks amazed, then runs for some more.
Sprinkles of laughter, a dash of delight,
In a world full of quirks, everything feels right.

The mailman slips, he's doing a jig,
While neighbors all laugh at the sight of the pig.
An umbrella flies off, sails high in the air,
Creating a scene so ridiculous, rare.

Whimsy bursts forth from the cracks in our day,
Brightening moments in the silliest way.
So grab all your giggles, hold tight to your fun,
For life's just a joke that's just begun!

Sarcasm in the Sunlight

Good morning, dear sun, you're blazing too bright,
The world's waking up, it's a comical sight.
The plants are all wilting, wishing for shade,
While birds sing their songs, oh what a charade.

A squirrel in a tie is running for fame,
Planning his breakfast with serious aim.
He steals all our nuts, thinks he's quite the boss,
In the kingdom of jesters, he's the one at a loss.

The ice cream truck's ringing, it's music divine,
But I'm on a diet—oh, how will I dine?
I'll grab me a cone made of pure, sweet regret,
With flavors of laughter I'll never forget.

In this sunlight of sarcasm, we find our roles,
Playing the jesters while laughing with souls.
So let's not forget this whimsical spree,
With a wink and a smirk, we can just be free!

The Art of Laughing at Ourselves

Stumbled on laughter, tripped on a pun,
Caught in the act of forgetting the fun.
With shoes that don't match and hair in a mess,
We laugh at our quirks, embrace all the stress.

The mirror reflects that ridiculous face,
With cheesecake and crumbs, it's a brand-new embrace.
For in every blunder, there's magic to find,
A giggle's the glue that binds heart and mind.

We dance like the world is a giant big joke,
Each silly mistake, a fine radius stroke.
With friends who can chuckle at life's little tricks,
We spin through the chaos, making our picks.

So raise up your glass to the folly we share,
For in our own laughter, we find we can care.
The art of this giggle, so bright and so bold,
Is the treasure we seek, worth more than gold.

Tickles of Truth

A dog with a squeaker is quite the loud cheer,
For truth in the chaos is sweeter than beer.
The birds whistle tunes that are just out of key,
But somehow their chorus feels perfect to me.

With socks that don't match and a hat that won't stay,
We find the sweet humor in life's playful fray.
The truth is a tickle that lights up our souls,
A giggle that rolls as absurdity rolls.

When life throws a curveball, we dodge and we weave,
With laughter as armor, there's nothing to grieve.
We share in our foibles, embrace every gaffe,
It's the tickles of truth that make us both laugh.

So come join the dance, be silly and bright,
For humor's the lantern that lights up our night.
In a world that is wacky, our spirits will soar,
With tickles of truth, we can always want more!

Laughter's Lullaby

In the morning's gentle light,
A clumsy cat takes flight.
It tumbles down, a soft thud,
While giggles rise like warm, sweet buds.

With every slip and silly dance,
A chance to share a bouncy glance.
So laugh away the dreary gray,
And let joy lead the way.

The Lighthearted Lens

Through a silly pair of specs,
The world is bright, any vex.
A chicken struts with goofy flair,
As onlookers stop and stare.

In every joke, a spark ignites,
Bouncing laughter through the nights.
Oh, how life wears a playful grin,
With laughter dancing on the skin.

Gags of the Galaxy

In a spaceship zooming far and wide,
An alien drops his cola, what a ride!
With bubbly chaos swirling 'round,
Their giggles echo through the sound.

Rocket raccoons throwing pies,
As stardust glimmers in their eyes.
Each cosmic joke, a starry jest,
Bringing laughter, truly the best.

Snickers in the Silence

In the stillness of the night,
A sneaky mouse steals a bite.
With a chunk of cheese in sight,
He prances off with pure delight.

Every snicker breaks the calm,
As chuckles rise, a healing balm.
Even shadows have their fun,
In their whispers, laughter's spun.

The Symphony of Silly

In a world where penguins dance,
A cat wears shades, taking a chance.
Llamas in top hats play the tune,
While chickens moonwalk under the moon.

Giraffes in sneakers run a race,
Balloons take flight with joyful grace.
A dog in socks plays fetch with style,
And giggles echo for quite a while.

Pies that fly and jokes that trip,
And donuts tossed on a comical slip.
In this wild world of laughter's reign,
Every moment is bright, never plain.

So grab your hat and join the swing,
Let's dance and laugh, let joy take wing.
For silly things make spirits soar,
A symphony of smiles, forevermore.

Witty Wanderings

A squirrel wears glasses, reading a book,
While frogs in suits do a double take look.
The bees wear ties, buzzing in thrall,
As ants do the conga, having a ball.

Down the path where mischief brews,
A turtle races—a runaway snooze!
With breadcrumbs tossed like confetti bright,
The wildest adventures unfold in delight.

Jokes stroll leisurely, arm in arm,
Spreading giggles and harmless charm.
A rainbow of laughter in every zone,
Witty wanderings, never alone.

So pack your giggles and share them wide,
In this quirky journey, let joy be your guide.
With every step, there's humor to find,
On this trail of smiles that's one of a kind.

Humor's Hidden Treasures

Hidden in cracks where the laughter leaks,
Is a sock that dances and tickles our cheeks.
A treasure map leading to giggles galore,
With each silly step, we discover more.

A parrot in feathers, spouting wisecracks,
As cats play cards and occasionally relax.
The chest of joy holds jests and puns,
And life's little quirks that shine like suns.

Discover the gems buried below,
Where joy sprouts from the smallest hello.
Glittering in laughter, it lights up the night,
In humor's trove, everything feels right.

So dig through the moments, find the delight,
In the whims of the day, from morning to night.
For treasure's not gold; it's the laugh we share,
Hidden in life's playful, whimsical care.

Life's Playful Puzzles

A jigsaw blitz with pieces misled,
A cat in a hat, showing its head.
Puzzles that giggle, twist, and confound,
In each quirky corner, more laughter is found.

A riddle from squirrels, a ticklish chase,
While ducks practice yoga and find their grace.
The solution's a smile, simple and bright,
In the game of life, humor takes flight.

Crossword capers where answers are silly,
A laugh at the end, making all feel frilly.
Each twist and turn leads to delight,
A playful dance in the soft moonlight.

So piece it together with joy as the glue,
Every puzzle unravels, revealing what's true.
In laughter's embrace, let us confidently stride,
For life's playful puzzles bring joy as our guide.

Giggles at the Edge of Sorrow

Life's a dance with silly shoes,
Stumbling on both highs and blues.
Laughter lingers in the air,
Tickles hiding everywhere.

Jokes are buried like a bone,
In the marrow of our own.
Even tears can wear a grin,
With a snort or silly spin.

Puns are flung like paper planes,
Sailing through our joys and pains.
Each wisecrack's a gentle nudge,
Reminding us to never judge.

So let's toast to the absurd,
Raise a glass, let laughter be heard.
In the chaos, find your tune,
As the sun dances with the moon.

Quirks of Existence

Life's a riddle wrapped in jest,
Finding joy is quite the quest.
Watch the cat chase its own tail,
In that chase, we cannot fail.

Sneezes echo in the breeze,
Turning heads with playful ease.
Slip on butter, bump a knee,
Oh, the tales that come to be!

Coffee spills, a morning craze,
Seeing clumsiness ablaze.
We trip through paths of light and shade,
Every stumble, yet unswayed.

In the circus of our days,
Fun and laughter lightly plays.
With a chuckle, we shall roam,
Finding humor—this is home.

Smiles in the Shadows

In the gloom, a wink appears,
Waves hello to doubts and fears.
Life's a comedy of errors,
Where joy sprouts from hidden terrors.

Silly hats on serious heads,
Make the mundane just like threads.
Witty banter in the dark,
Bonds are built and laughter's spark.

Even ducks with silly quacks,
Teach us how to pause, relax.
Falling down can lead to grace,
Spinning smiles on every face.

So if shadows close around,
Turn the frown right upside down.
In each moment, find the thrill,
With a giggle, we fulfill.

The Jester's Guide to Living

Jesters juggle truth and jest,
Turning trials to a fest.
In a world so stern and gray,
Bring your laughter into play.

Wear mismatched socks with pride,
Dance where serious folks would hide.
Twist your tongue in silly rhymes,
Embrace laughter through the times.

Every blunder's just a chance,
For a spontaneous dance.
Through the cracks, we find delight,
In the chaos, we take flight.

So grab a moment, sprinkle cheer,
Life's too short to live in fear.
With a wink and grin, we'll thrive,
In this circus, we'll arrive.

Tickling the Surface of Reality

A chicken crossed the road one day,
To ask the duck, 'What's your play?'
With feathers bright and a quack so loud,
They formed a duo, strangely proud.

The clock chimed twelve, the fish did dance,
A cat in a hat thought it a chance.
They twirled and jumped, under the sun,
Reality bent, just a bit of fun.

Two squirrels debated: nuts or cheese?
While ants marched by with effortless ease.
A butterfly giggled, took to the sky,
Life's absurdities make laughter fly.

With each small jest, the world feels light,
Turned upside down, the moon shines bright.
So let's embrace this wacky spree,
Tickling truth, wild and free!

Finding Joy in the Mundane

An old toaster popped up with some bread,
It squealed out loud, 'I'm not done yet!'
The coffee pot danced with glee,
Saying, 'Wake up! Come sip on me!'

On rainy days, the socks played chess,
While pencils rolled with a simple finesse.
A paperclip formed a human chain,
Binding together through laughter and strain.

Each task mundane turned upside down,
A dust bunny spun, twirled like a clown.
The broom took a ride, you should see!
In every corner, joy roams free.

So let's savor the small, with a wink and a grin,
For in every moment, the giggles begin.
Life's little quirks, we can adore,
Finding joy in the things we bore!

The Playful Heart

A heart once heavy tripped on a shoe,
It laughed so hard, the world felt new.
With every beat, it danced along,
To a silly tune, a playful song.

In a meadow bright, a bug wore shades,
Sipping on dew, throwing fun parades.
The sun joined in, with a bright, warm grin,
As the clouds giggled, letting joy spin.

With a wiggle and jiggle, the grass stood tall,
While daisies whispered, 'Let's have a ball!'
A feather took flight, teasing the breeze,
Brewing up laughter, like a tease.

Let's cherish the things that lift us high,
With playful hearts, we'll learn to fly.
In this wacky world, let's take our part,
Embracing the laughter of a playful heart!

Jokes on Our Journey

A tortoise raced with a hare on track,
But tripped on a rock, oh what a quack!
They stumbled and laughed, no worries near,
'Let's take our time, there's nothing to fear!'

With each mile ticked, a joke was spun,
The map got lost, but oh, what fun!
A snail in a hat claimed he was fast,
While the wind whispered tales of the past.

They stopped for a snack, shared crumbs and glee,
Even a tree joined, swaying happily.
With each twist and turn, their joy would grow,
Cherishing moments, taking it slow.

So laugh through the detours, dance in the rain,
For life's little jests are never in vain.
On this grand journey, let humor be king,
With jokes as our compass, it's a beautiful thing!

Lighthearted Musings Amidst Chaos

In the midst of the rush, I trip on my shoe,
The world laughs with me, not at me, it's true.
Why worry and fret when the sky's painted blue?
Let's dance in the rain, let the giggles ensue.

I spilled my coffee, a glorious mess,
Paper towels crumbled, oh what a stress!
Yet here comes the laughter, I must confess,
In life's little blunders, there's joy to assess.

When the kids run around, it's quite the circus,
Their laughter ignites a sweet, gentle purpose.
A pie in the face, although it seems burdensome,
It's moments like these that keep us feeling young.

Why take things too seriously, it's all a jest,
The cat steals my sandwich, isn't he the best?
With humor as my compass, I feel so blessed,
In a world full of chaos, I find my zest.

A Dose of Delight

When life throws a curveball, just give it a wink,
With a shrug of the shoulders, it makes you rethink.
A tickle on Tuesdays can make the heart sink,
A giggle or two, and your spirits will blink.

Stumbling in shoes that are two sizes small,
I wobble and stumble, but who cares at all?
A parade of chuckles, a never-ending sprawl,
With humor my armor, I stand proud and tall.

Frogs dressed as princes on this winding road,
With laughter our currency, it lightens the load.
Silly moments like these are joys to be sowed,
In the garden of life, let them brightly explode.

Laughing at Life's Puzzling Path

Life's like a riddle with missing pieces,
I puzzle with laughter as small chaos increases.
When things go amiss, the humor releases,
Like jesters in court, we dance like wild leases.

The dog wears a hat, the cat's in a vest,
They prance through the garden, putting joy to the test.
A fumble in speech, yet I feel so blessed,
In the art of the chuckle, I find my zest.

When plans start to wobble like jelly on toast,
I giggle and grin, not fretting the most.
For in all the madness, it's laughter I boast,
In the puzzle of life, humor is the host.

Serenade of the Smirk

A wink from the past, a nudge from today,
Life's quirks and its twists, they're here to stay.
With smirks in abundance, they light up the way,
It's laughter that guides us, come what may.

I tripped over puns that rolled off my tongue,
Each moment a jest, I feel forever young.
In the jazz of existence, laughter is sung,
With joy as the melody, I'm gladly sprung.

A facial expression, a tickle, a grin,
In the game of life's humor, we all win.
With mischief and giggles, let the fun begin,
In this serenade of smirks, let the light in.

A Comedy of Everyday Affairs

In the kitchen, pots do clatter,
As I search for the spatula on the platter.
The bread pops up, my toast is rare,
Burnt on one side, but who would care?

The sock drawer fights, they never match,
A game of hide and seek, a tricky catch.
I step outside, it starts to rain,
My umbrella's inside, oh, life's a pain!

The cat's in the box, the dog steals the chair,
Who needs a quiet home when chaos is there?
The phone rings loud, I leap in fright,
It's just a friend—let's laugh tonight!

So here's to the quirks that make us grin,
The little mishaps we tuck right in.
Life's a stage, we play our parts,
With humor, we mend our funny hearts.

The Dance of the Slightly Silly

The cat wore a hat, it looked so grand,
While I tripped over shoes I'd left unplanned.
With silly socks and mismatched ties,
We stumble through laughter and blurry skies.

A pie on my face, a laugh with the kids,
In the park, it's less about the bids.
We spin and twirl like leaves on a breeze,
A dance of the silly, with utter ease.

Giggles erupt from the oddest of places,
Like when grandma shows up in wild braces.
With each kooky tale that does unfold,
Life shines brighter than silver or gold.

So let's twirl around, in a madcap spree,
As the world spins round with glee, oh me!
We'll laugh at the slips, the unexpected turns,
For in each little moment, true joy returns.

Laugh Lines through the Years

With every wrinkle comes a tale,
Like the time I lost my shoe on the trail.
A road trip mishap, with snacks all gone,
We laughed till we cried, dusk to dawn.

At fifty, my hair has a bit more flair,
The kids tease me, 'Dad, what's that up there?'
I chuckle and say, 'It's my wisdom crown!'
As I trip on the rug, and tumble down.

Those family dinners packed tight with cheer,
When Uncle Joe's stories bring laughter near.
We toast to the moments, the blunders, the slips,
And giggle at tears from those laughing trips.

Looking back, I treasure each silly fight,
Each chuckle, each giggle, each joyful insight.
For life in its laughter is truly sublime,
Creating sweet lines through the fabric of time.

Beneath the Weight of a Giggle

When Mondays arrive with the weight of a yawn,
I stumble through breakfast like a zombie at dawn.
The coffee spills over, it mimics my brain,
A snort escapes as I feel the pain.

At work, a memo brings a chuckle or two,
'Please avoid using hijinks in the queue.'
The printer jams, a paper monster lurks,
As I dance my way through my goofy quirks.

The bus arrives late, I slip in the rain,
With every adventure, there's laughter to gain.
A smile from a stranger can lighten the load,
As we share our follies on this rocky road.

So let's not forget when the days feel long,
To laugh at our lives, right where we belong.
For beneath every burden, there's joy we reveal,
In laughter entwined, oh, life's the real deal!

Smiles in the Mundane

A dog in a tutu, prancing with glee,
Chasing its tail like a wild jubilee.
A cat in a box, thinks it's a spaceship,
Zooming through life on a serious trip.

The guy in the office with socks that don't match,
Swears he's a trendsetter; his colleagues just scratch.
The spilled coffee dance, a marvelous sight,
Laughter erupts as he clumsily bites.

The neighbor who mows in a sparkly hat,
Looks like a disco on a Sunday chat.
Each day is a puzzle, strange pieces unfold,
Filling the frames of our lives to behold.

With winks and odd quirks, embrace what you find,
In every small moment, let joy be aligned.
From chuckles to snorts, let your spirit take flight,
In the canvas of life, colors sparkle so bright.

Chuckles Over Coffee

Gathered with friends, cups clinking in cheer,
Sipping on laughter, it's music we hear.
The barista's a joker, with jokes up his sleeve,
Serving up smiles, it's hard to believe.

Stringing our stories as sugar's poured in,
Each tale gets taller, let the giggles begin.
With each little sip, woes fade to the side,
In a world brewed of laughter, there's nothing to hide.

Cream spilled on the table, a sight so absurd,
The laughter erupts, as our spirits are stirred.
A toast to the moments, both silly and bright,
In the warmth of our friendship, the world feels just right.

So let's raise our mugs, fill them to the brim,
With joy and with laughter, let our hearts swim.
In the game of humor, we'll never be lone,
For chuckles over coffee make us feel at home.

The Lightness of Being Quirky

Worn-out shoes dancing, untamed by the laces,
They skip through the pavement with comical graces.
A hat with a feather, tall as it can be,
Fluffs up the mood like a big cup of tea.

Cloudy the cat, with a penchant for socks,
Snoozes in slippers, loves cozy knocks.
Giggles from children, they share funny dreams,
Imagining worlds where nothing's as it seems.

Life's like a circus, all colors and fun,
With clowns and tightropes beneath the bright sun.
Each blunder, a treasure, each mishap, a cheer,
With quirks in our pockets, we've nothing to fear.

Embrace all the oddities, dance with the strange,
For joy wears a mask, a delightful exchange.
In a world of the quirky, let's lift up our hearts,
Each laugh a reminder of sweet, silly parts.

Giggles Beyond the Gloom

When rain clouds gather, and shadows draw near,
A kid jumps in puddles, ignoring his fear.
Umbrellas that flip over, strange outfits they wear,
Laughter takes charge, chasing woe from the air.

The grumpy old grinch with his cat on a sail,
Whiskered and wobbly, they set off on a trail.
With every snort, chuckles ripple like waves,
Even the night's sighs, want joy to behave.

The moon pulls a prank, brightening the dark,
While shadows play tag, giggling through the park.
In moments of chaos, let laughter ignite,
For in every chuckle, there's hope taking flight.

So march through the gloom, with a grin on your face,
Find joy in the quirks; let your heart feel its grace.
For even the rainy, the dreary, the gray,
Hold treasure and laughter, come what may.